THE ESSENTIAL JEROME KERN SONG BOOK

WISE PUBLICATIONS
LONDON/NEW YORK/SYDNEY

EXCLUSIVE DISTRIBUTORS:
MUSIC SALES LIMITED
8/9 FRITH STREET, LONDON W1V 5TZ, ENGLAND.
MUSIC SALES PTY LIMITED
120 ROTHSCHILD AVENUE, ROSEBERY, NSW 2018, AUSTRALIA.

THIS BOOK © COPYRIGHT 1990 BY WISE PUBLICATIONS
ORDER NO.AM81506
UK ISBN 0.7119.2385.X

DESIGNED BY PEARCE MARCHBANK STUDIO
ARRANGED BY FRANK BOOTH
MUSIC PROCESSED BY BILL PITT

MUSIC SALES' COMPLETE CATALOGUE LISTS THOUSANDS OF TITLES AND IS
FREE FROM YOUR LOCAL MUSIC SHOP, OR DIRECT FROM MUSIC SALES LIMITED.
PLEASE SEND £1.75 IN STAMPS FOR POSTAGE TO MUSIC SALES LIMITED,
8/9 FRITH STREET, LONDON W1V 5TZ.

A FINE ROMANCE

MUSIC BY JEROME KERN
WORDS BY DOROTHY FIELDS

She: (1) A fine ro - mance! with no kiss - es! A fine ro - mance, my friend,

She: (2) (A) fine ro - mance! my good fel - low! You take ro - mance, I'll take

He: (3) (A) fine ro - mance! with no kiss - es! A fine ro - mance, my friend

He: (4) (A) fine ro - mance! my dear Duch - ess! Two old fo - gies who need

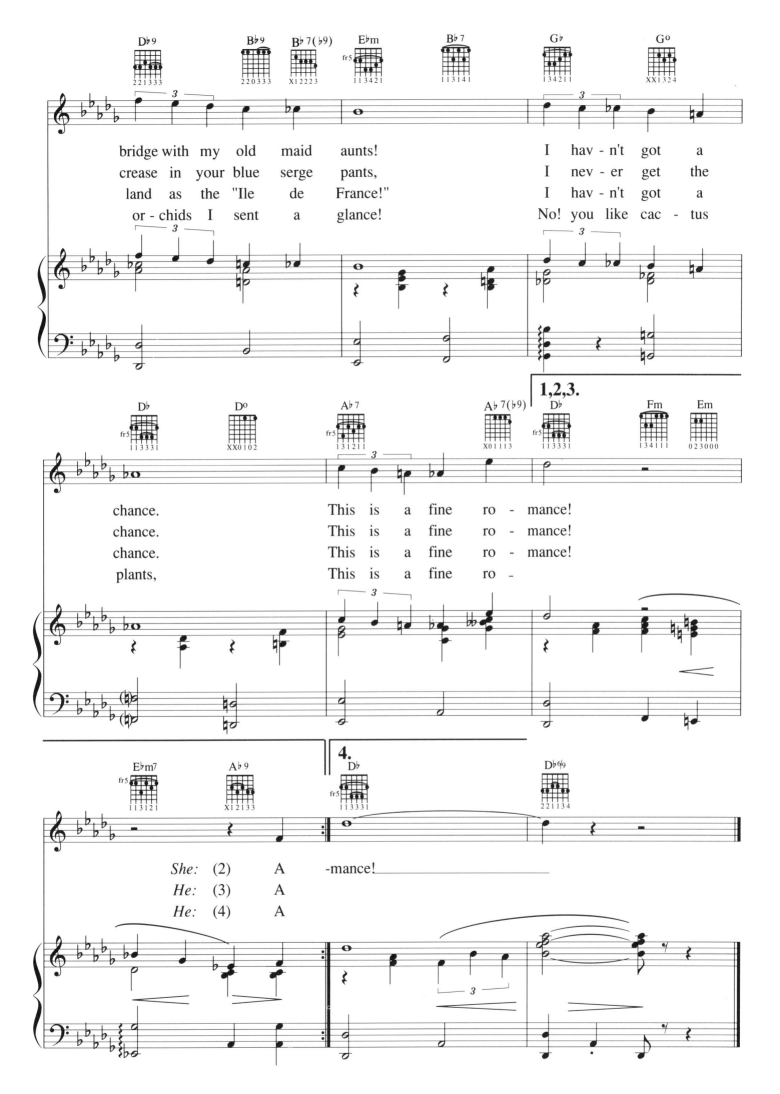

ALL THE THINGS YOU ARE

MUSIC BY JEROME KERN
WORDS BY OSCAR HAMMERSTEIN II

Moderately, with expression

You

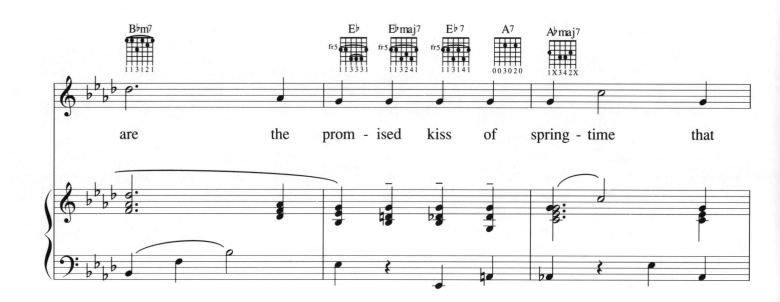

are   the prom - ised kiss of spring - time that

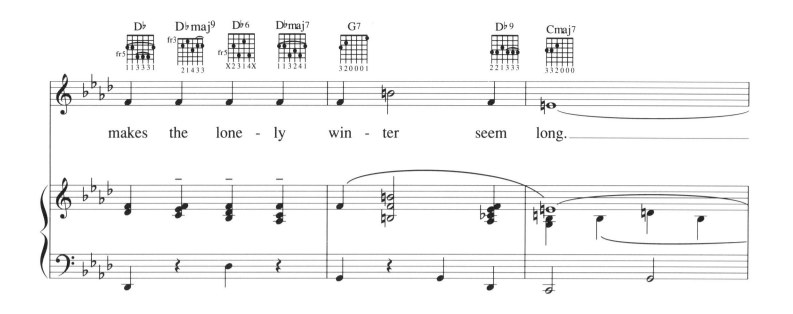

makes the lone - ly win - ter seem long. _____

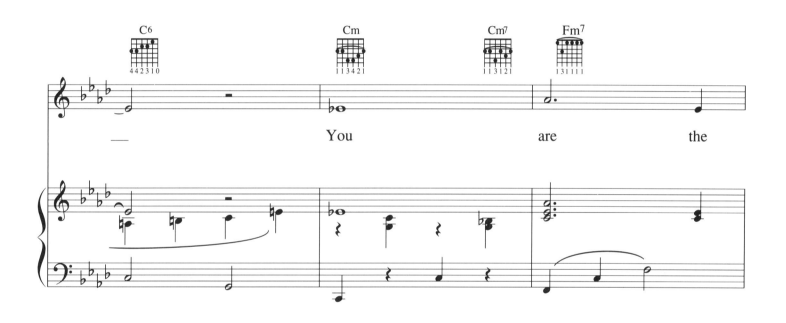

_____ You are the

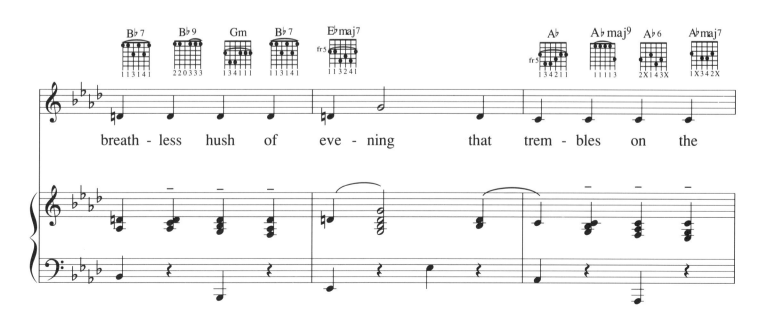

breath - less hush of eve - ning that trem - bles on the

brink of a love - ly song.＿＿＿＿＿＿＿＿＿＿＿ You are the

ang - el glow＿＿＿ that lights a star,＿＿＿＿＿＿＿＿＿＿＿

＿ the dear - est things I know＿＿ are what you

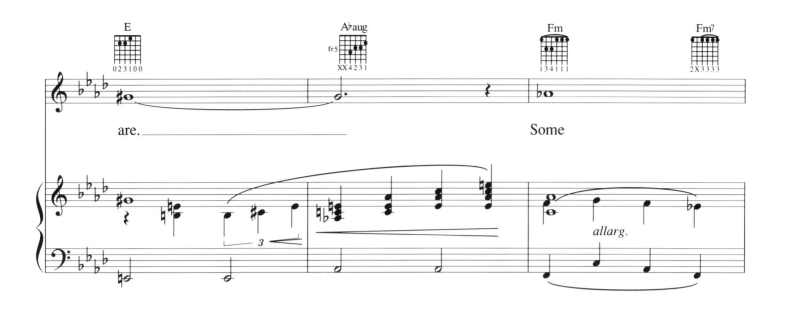

are. _____ Some

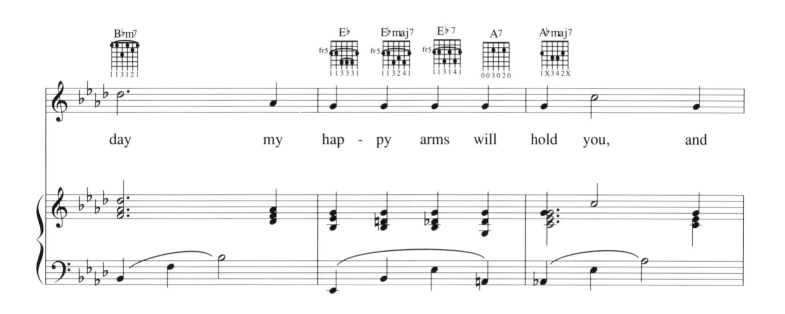

day my hap - py arms will hold you, and

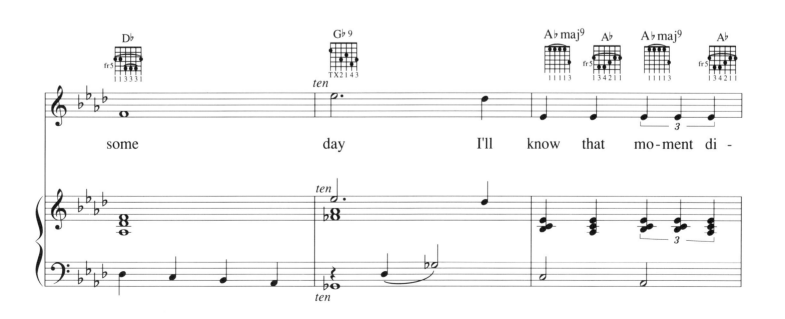

some day I'll know that mo - ment di -

vine,   when   all   the   things   you   are,   are

1. mine!

2. mine! _____

BILL

MUSIC BY JEROME KERN
WORDS BY P. G. WODEHOUSE & OSCAR HAMMERSTEIN II

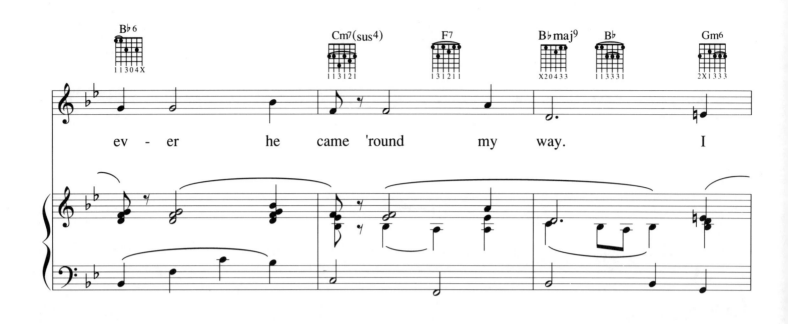

ev - er he came 'round my way.   I

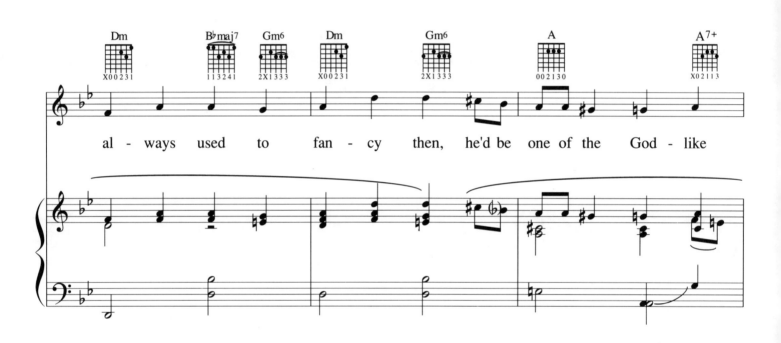

al - ways used to fan - cy then, he'd be one of the God - like

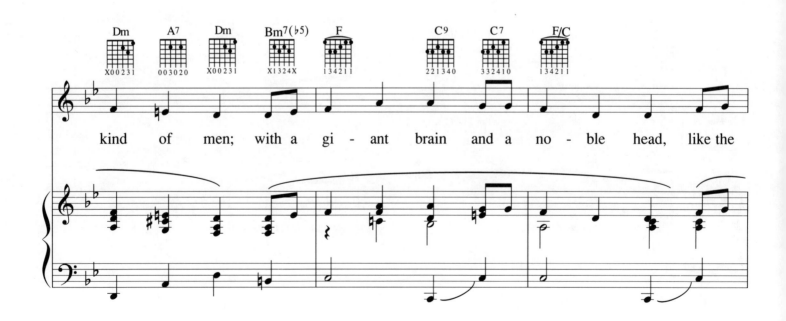

kind of men; with a gi - ant brain and a no - ble head, like the

makes   me   thrill.   I   love   him_____   be - cause he's
makes   me   thrill.   I   love   him_____   be - cause he's

won - der - ful,_____   be - cause he's   just   my
I   don't know,_____   be - cause he's   just   my

1.   **2.**

Bill_____   (2)He's   Bill.

molto rall.

17

CAN'T HELP LOVIN' DAT MAN

MUSIC BY JEROME KERN
WORDS BY OSCAR HAMMERSTEIN II

When he goes a - way   dat's a rain - y

piu mosso e cresc.

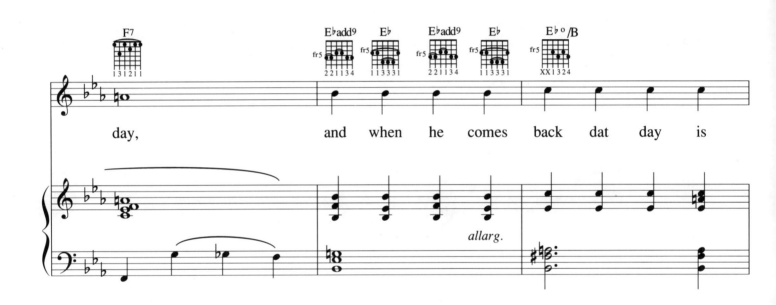

day,   and when he comes back dat day is

allarg.

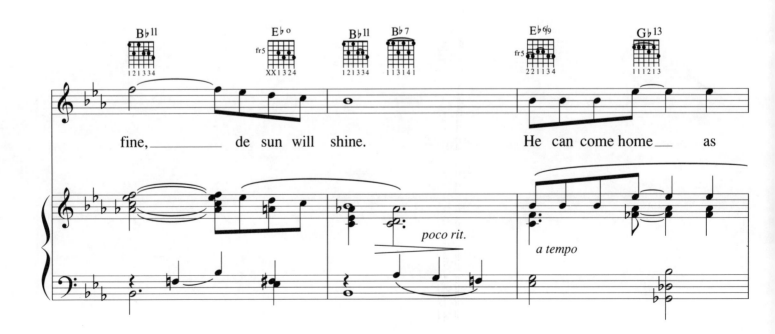

fine,_____ de sun will shine.   He can come home___ as

poco rit.   *a tempo*

late as can be,___ home wid-out him___ ain't no home to me,

Can't help lov-in' dat man___ of mine.

mine.___

LONG AGO AND FAR AWAY

MUSIC BY JEROME KERN
WORDS BY IRA GERSHWIN

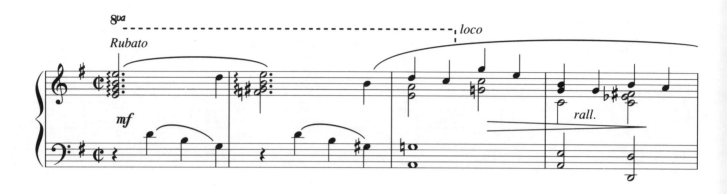

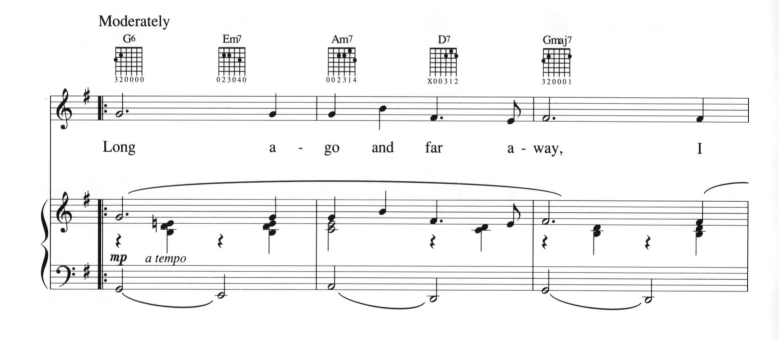

Long a - go and far a - way, I

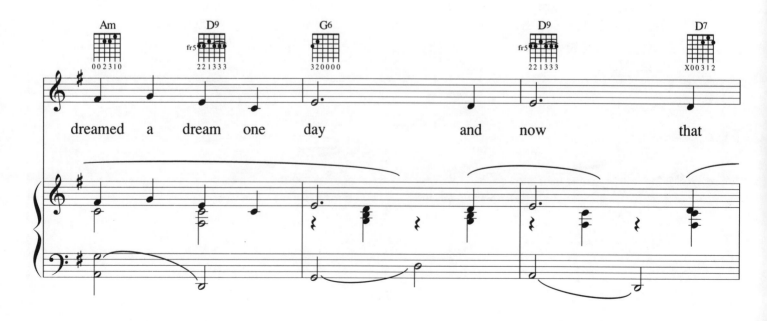

dreamed a dream one day and now that

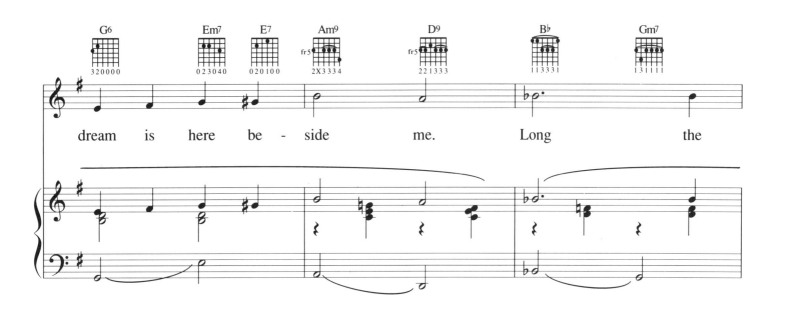

dream is here be - side me. Long the

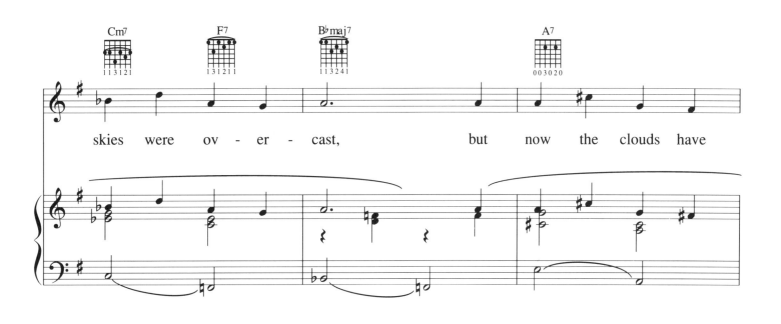

skies were ov - er - cast, but now the clouds have

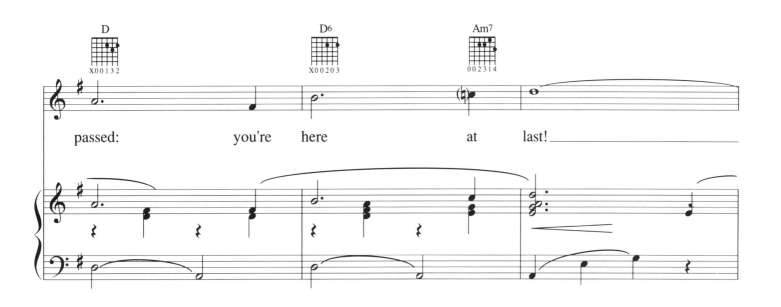

passed: you're here at last! _____

Just one look and then I knew _____ that all I longed for long a-go was

1. you.

2. you. _____

OL' MAN RIVER
MUSIC BY JEROME KERN
WORDS BY OSCAR HAMMERSTEIN II

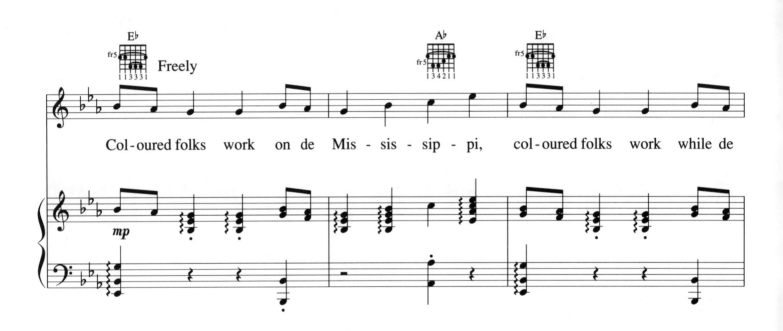

Col-oured folks work on de Mis - sis - sip - pi, col-oured folks work while de

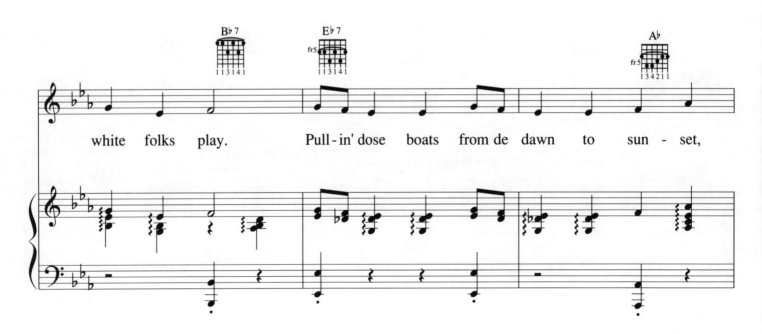

white folks play. Pull-in' dose boats from de dawn to sun - set,

git-tin' no rest till de judge-ment day. Don't look up 'an

don't look down, you don't dast make de white boss frown; Bend yo' knees an'

bow yo' head, an' pull dat rope un-til you're dead. Let me go 'way from de

Mis - sis - sip - pi, let me go 'way from de white men boss.

Show me dat stream called de riv - er Jor - dan, dat's de 'ol stream dat I

long to cross. _____

REFRAIN (Very slowly, with expression)

Ol' man riv - er, dat ol' man riv - er, He

must know sump-in', but don't say noth-in', He jus' keeps roll-in', He

keeps on roll-in' a-long._____ He don't plant 'ta-ters, he

don't plant cot-ton, an' dem dat plants 'em is soon for-got-ten; But ol' man riv-er, he

29

sick of try-in', Ah'm tired of liv-in' an' skeered of dy-in', but

ol' man riv-er, he jus' keeps roll-in' a - long.

long.

PICK YOURSELF UP
MUSIC BY JEROME KERN
WORDS BY DOROTHY FIELDS

Noth - ing's im-poss-i-ble I have found, for when my chin is

on the ground, I pick my-self up, dust my-self off, start all o-ver a-

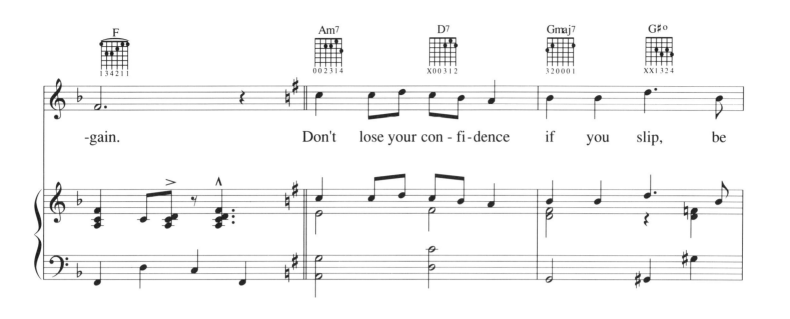

-gain.　　　　Don't　lose your con - fi -dence　if　you　slip,　be

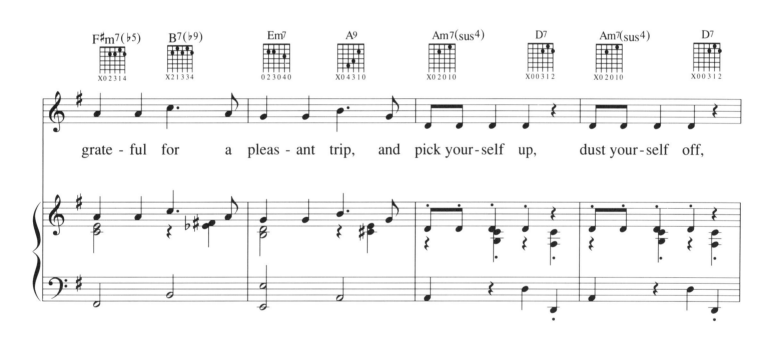

grate - ful　for　a　pleas - ant　trip,　and　pick your - self　up,　dust your - self　off,

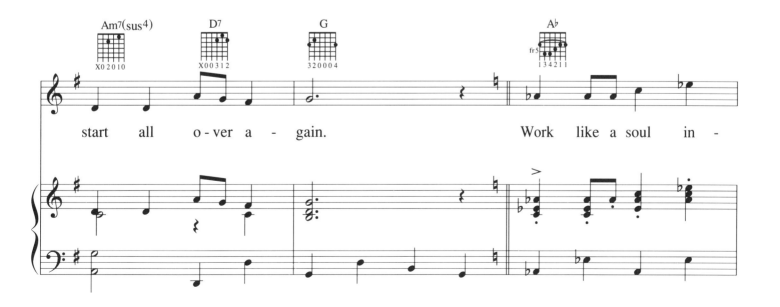

start　all　o - ver　a - gain.　　　　Work　like　a　soul　in -

-spir - ed,   till the bat-tle of the day is won.   You may be sick and

tir - ed,   but you'll be a man my son!   Will you re-mem-ber the

fa - mous men, who had to fall   to rise a - gain?   So take a deep breath,

SMOKE GETS IN YOUR EYES

MUSIC BY JEROME KERN
WORDS BY OTTO HARBACH

love.   Now   laugh-ing friends de - ride   tears I can-not

hide,_____   so I smile and say   "when a love-ly flame

dies,   smoke gets in your eyes."_____

THE FOLKS WHO LIVE ON THE HILL

MUSIC BY JEROME KERN
WORDS BY OSCAR HAMMERSTEIN II

as an-y fam' - ly will,_____ but we will al-ways be called_____

_____ "The folks who live on the hill"._____

Our_____ ve-ran-da will com-mand a view of mead-ows green,_____ the sort of

the folks who like to be called_____ what they have al-ways been called.

"The folks who live on the hill." ___

The Way You Look Tonight

MUSIC BY JEROME KERN
WORDS BY DOROTHY FIELDS

glow just think - ing of you,
for me but to love you,

and the way you look to - night. _____
just the way you look to - night. _____

1.
Oh, but you're

2.
With each

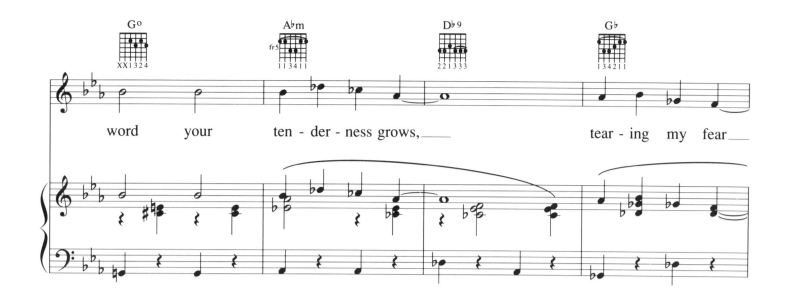

word your ten - der - ness grows,___ tear - ing my fear___

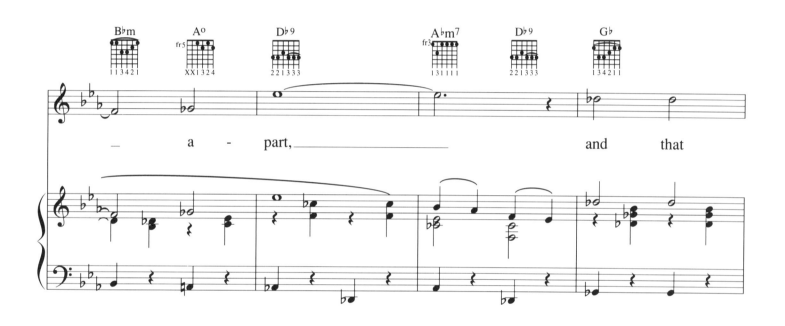

___ a - part,___ and that

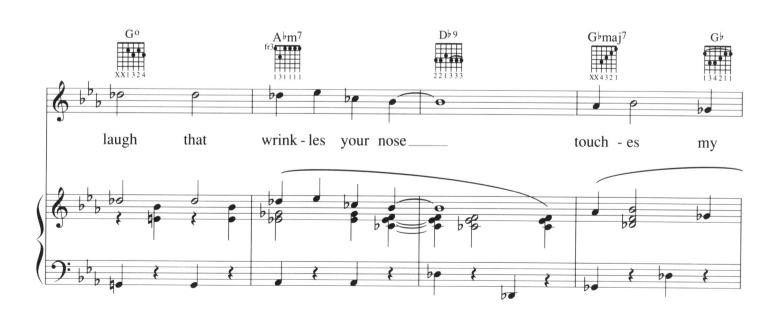

laugh that wrink - les your nose___ touch - es my

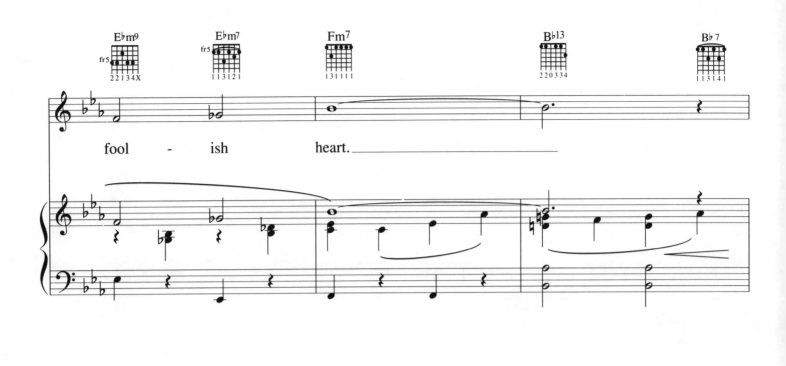

fool - ish heart._____

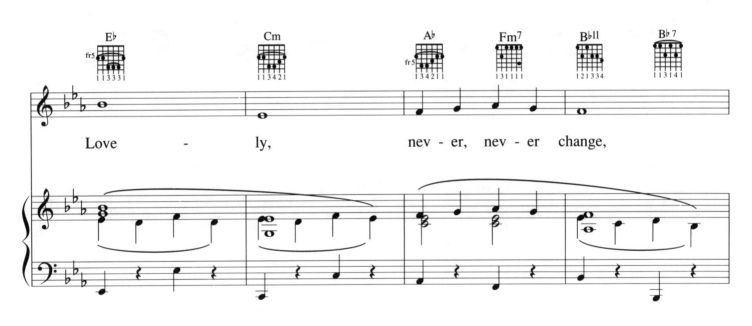

Love - ly, nev - er, nev - er change,

keep that breath-less charm, won't you please ar - range it, 'cause I

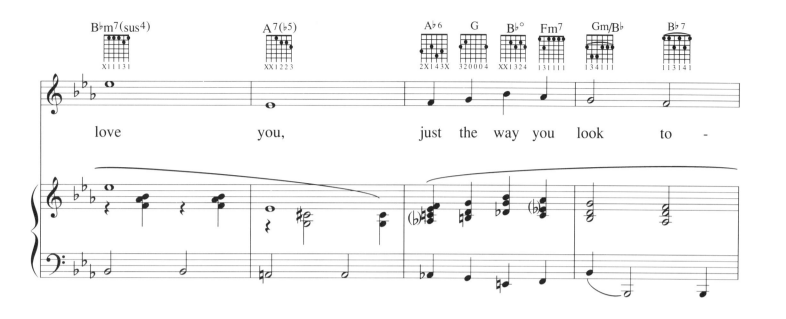

love you, just the way you look to -

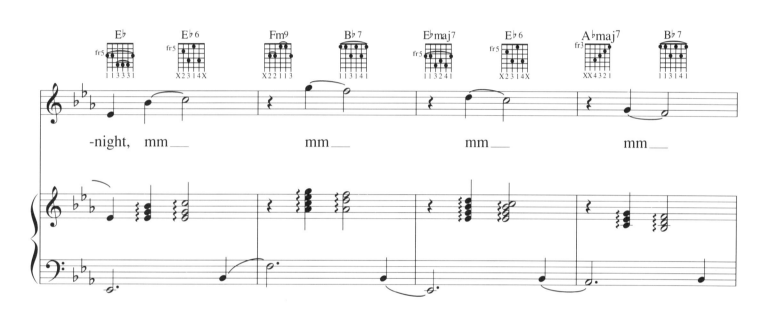

-night, mm___ mm___ mm___ mm___

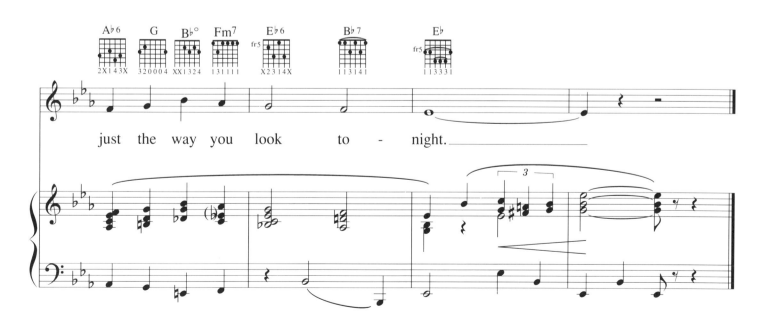

just the way you look to - night._____

THE LAST TIME I SAW PARIS

MUSIC BY JEROME KERN
WORDS BY OSCAR HAMMERSTEIN II

Moderately

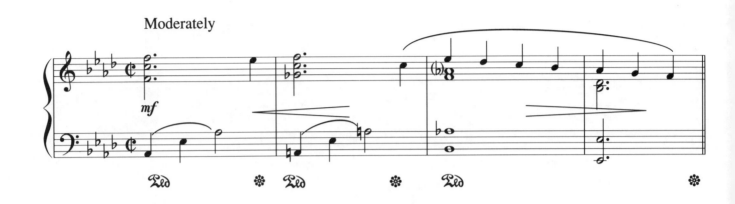

The last time I saw Par - is her heart was warm and

gay; I heard the laugh - ter of her heart in

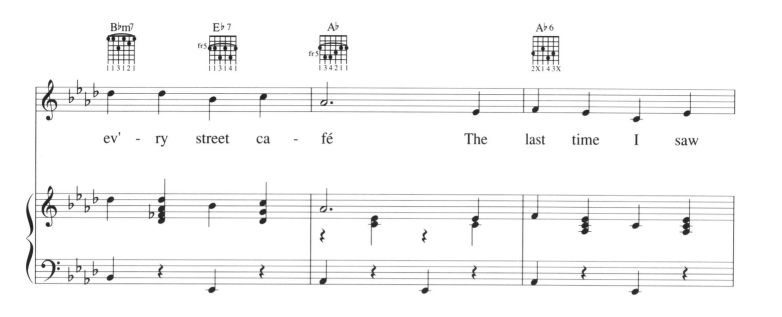

ev' - ry street ca - fé   The last time I saw

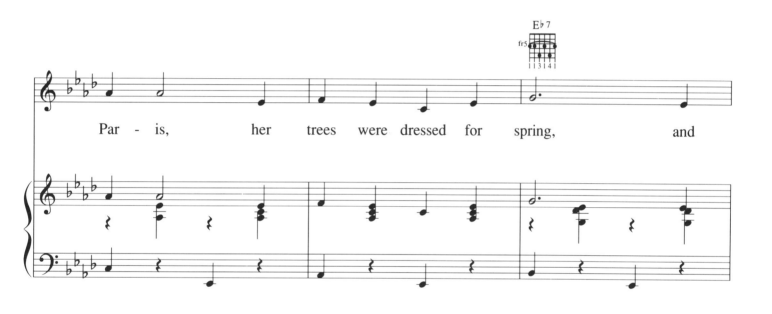

Par - is,   her   trees   were   dressed   for   spring,   and

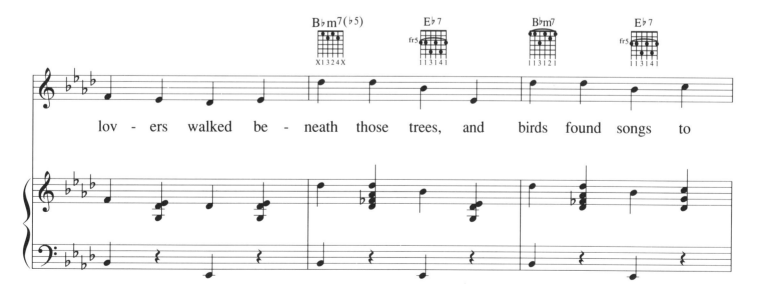

lov - ers   walked   be - neath   those   trees,   and   birds   found   songs   to

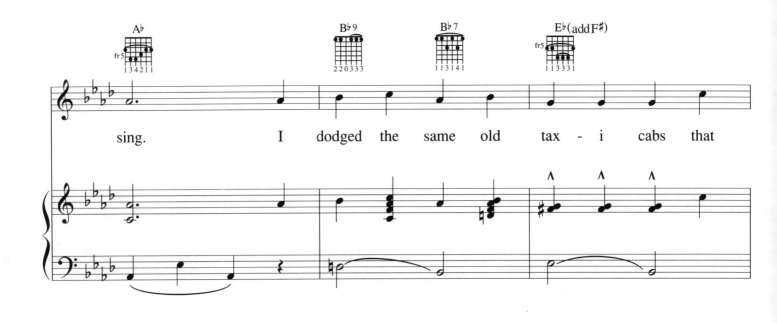

sing.   I dodged the same old tax - i cabs that

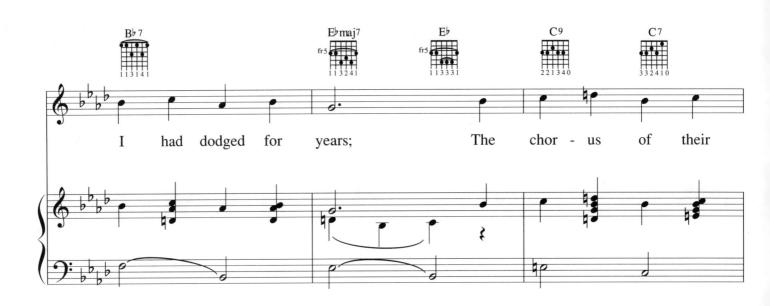

I had dodged for years;   The chor - us of their

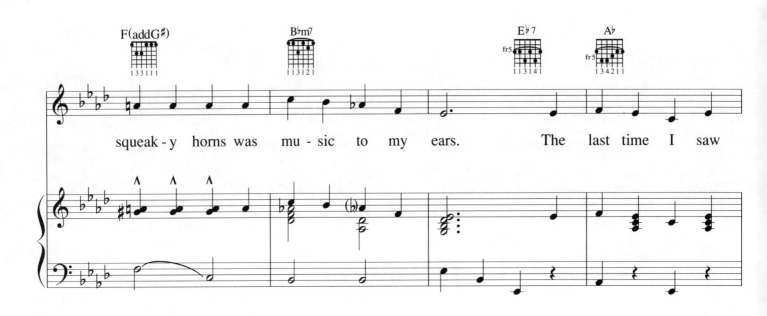

squeak - y horns was mu - sic to my ears.   The last time I saw

THE SONG IS YOU

MUSIC BY JEROME KERN
WORDS BY OSCAR HAMMERSTEIN II

Steady 2 beat

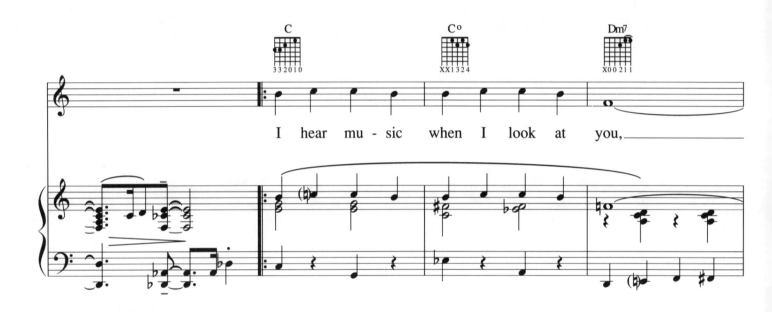

I hear mu-sic when I look at you,

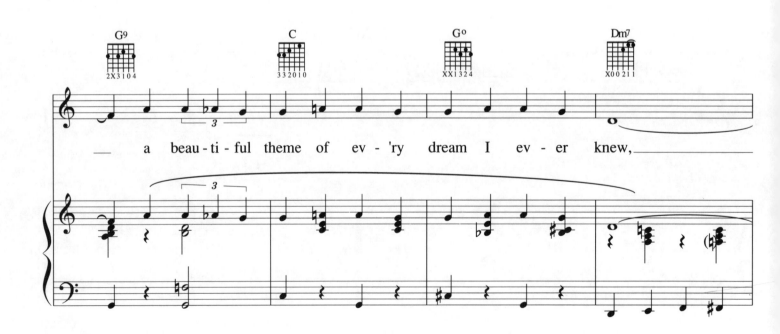

a beau-ti-ful theme of ev-'ry dream I ev-er knew,

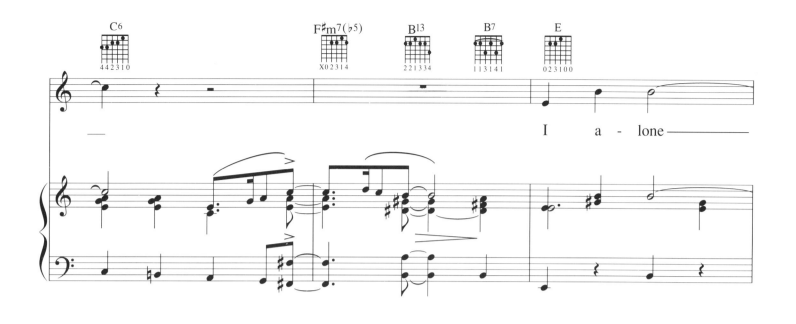

I a - lone————————

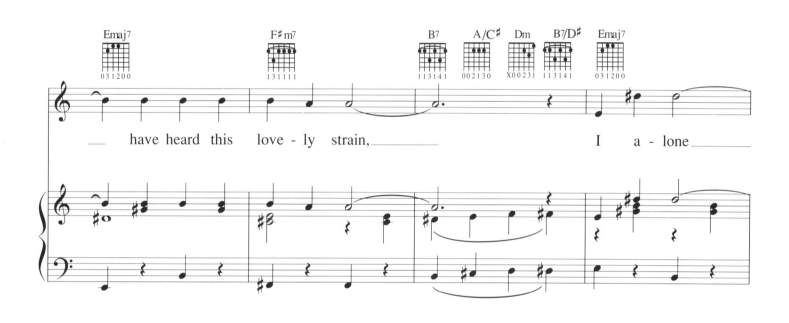

—— have heard this love - ly strain,————— I a - lone————

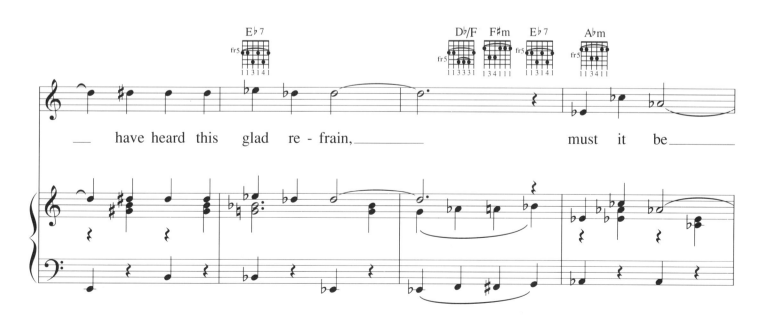

—— have heard this glad re - frain,————— must it be————

for - ev - er in - side of me, _____ why can't I

let it go, _____ why can't I let you know, _____ why can't I

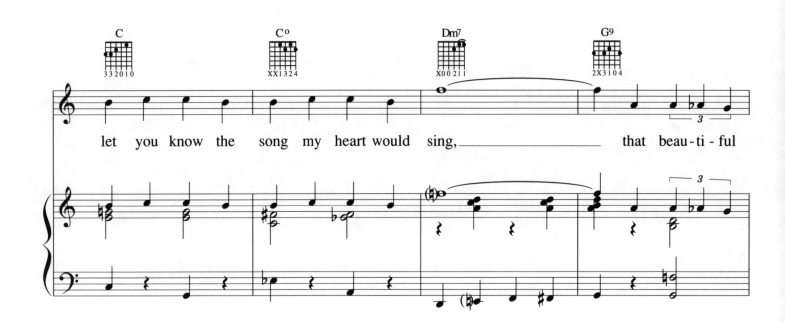

let you know the song my heart would sing, _____ that beau - ti - ful

THEY DIDN'T BELIEVE ME
MUSIC BY JEROME KERN
WORDS BY HERBERT REYNOLDS

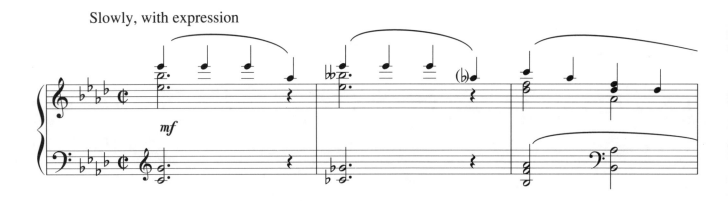

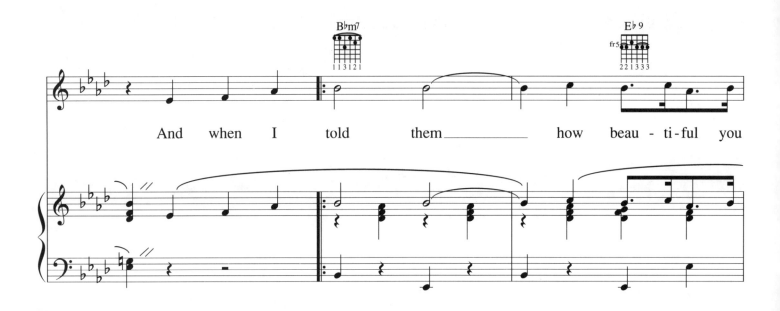

And when I told them _____ how beau-ti-ful you

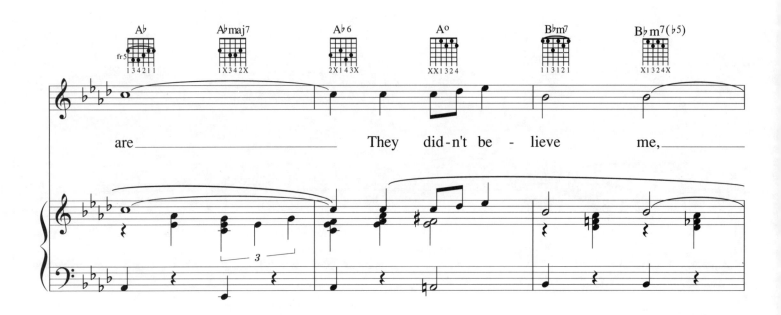

are _____ They did-n't be - lieve me, _____

And when I tell them,_____ and I cert'n-ly am goin' to

tell them,_____ that I'm the man whose

wife one day you'll be._____ They'll nev-er be -

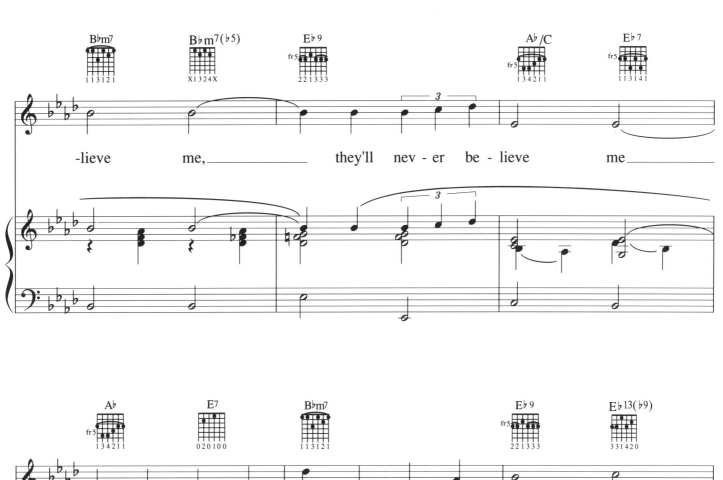

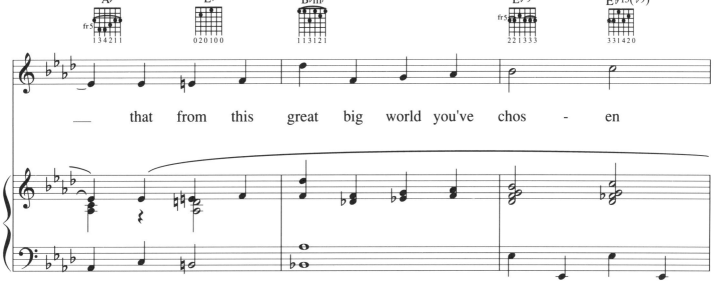

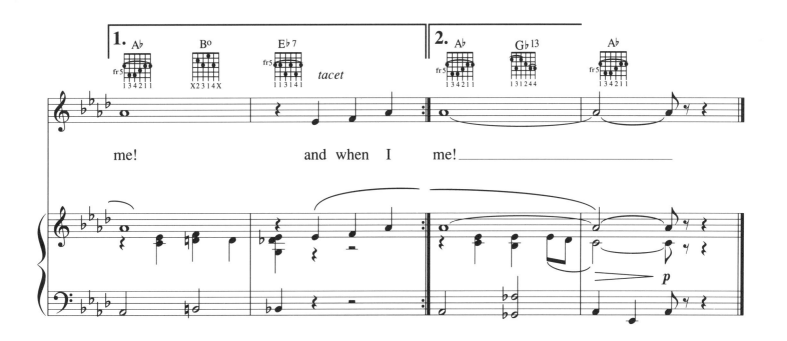

Printed and bound in Great Britain by
Caligraving Limited Thetford Norfolk

63

5/98 (30947)

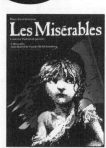

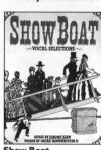